79/

5·11

12·1·24

RC

FINGERS
AND MOONS

Other books by the same author include:

A First Zen Reader
The Tiger's Cave
    (now retitled Second Zen Reader in its
    Japanese edition)
The Chapter of the Self
Zen and the Ways
Encounters in Yoga and Zen
The Warrior Koans
Śaṅkara on the Yoga-sūtra-s

FINGERS AND MOONS

A Collection of
Zen Stories and Incidents

by

TREVOR LEGGETT

BUDDHIST PUBLISHING GROUP
LEICESTER

Buddhist Publishing Group   PO Box 136
Leicester LE2 4TZ   England

British Library Cataloguing
in Publication Data

Leggett, Trevor
    Fingers and moons.
    1. Zen Buddhism
    I. Title
    294.3'927

    ISBN 0-946672-07-5

Printed in Great Britain by BPG

*To the late Dr Hari Prasad Shastri,
who introduced me to Zen
in its original Indian form,
these translations and comments are
reverently dedicated.*

CONTENTS

FOREWORD

This book is a transcript of talks given at the Summer School of the Buddhist Society in the years 1982 to 1985. I have in general kept the original colloquial presentation with its occasionally loose sentence construction. There were however a few cases where bare print could not convey the sense of a gesture or intonation, and extra words were therefore supplied.

Trevor Leggett
London, 1988

SPARKS FROM
THE HEART FLINT

SPARKS FROM
THE HEART FLINT

This talk is called *Sparks from the Heart Flint*. Of course our hearts aren't flinty — at least mine isn't — so in a way the whole basis of the talk collapses. But the fact is that other people (and sometimes they have good reason) think that my heart *is* flinty when you just scratch the surface. So for the purposes of my talk, the heart is a flint — it's hard and it can scratch. Now, when steel is applied skilfully to flint, a spark can be struck. If you've ever tried to do this, or seen it being done, you know that you don't get many sparks out of the striking with the steel — but you get some. And you have to go on until you get a spark.

Our heart flints can be struck in different ways, and one of the methods is to use short incidents and stories in the hope that one of them will sort of click. It's like trying to point out something in a distant landscape.

'You see that grey building with the round roof?'

'No, I can't make that out.'

Now you don't persist; you just say, 'Well, can you see the river gleaming in the distance?'

'No, no, I can't see it.'

You don't say, 'Well, you MUST see it!' You try something else. And sooner or later it comes. 'You see that red building on the far hill?'

'Yes, I've got that.'

'Now look at the red and go left, keep going left along the horizon and then you'll come to the green patch, and then you'll come to the river.' And so on.

So this style is connected with trying to get an initial spark and then going from there.

Our hearts have to be struck. These days the heart flint is generally regarded as the responsibility of society. If somebody does something wrong, well, in a way we're all guilty, aren't we, because we've set him a problem that he didn't really manage to overcome. The shepherd is guilty for not integrating the wolf with the flock, so to speak. But as a matter of fact, if we look at our own experience, we find that the idea of society being responsible is quite false. If I look at the spiteful and vicious things I've done, I can't honestly say that society was responsible — *I* did them! This is one of the first things to recognize — that the heart is a flint.

Then try applying these methods. They can be considered like jokes. Sometimes one sees a joke: it's enough. But if they don't see it, or if it's an inappropriate joke, or they've got no sense of humour, then it's no use labouring it — 'You *must* see this!' — or arguing about it. Just pass on to another one.

The next point comes when the spark is struck. You hold the flint in the left hand and you have some tinder, which is like dried grass, held on the flint under your left thumb. You strike, and the spark must catch the tinder, otherwise it's gone immediately. If it catches the tinder, you blow very very carefully, not too much, not too little; it'll glow, and you can light your cigarette or whatever it is. (It's a long way of lighting a cigarette: flint, steel, and tinder.) Now, these spiritual stories and incidents, and things that happen, they can strike a spark from us, but unless there's some tinder for it to catch, that spark is lost. We may feel a momentary exaltation, a momentary flash, and then it's gone. The tinder can be some persistent situation, some vivid past association, some fixed habit, some problem, or obsession. When that's struck, when the spark strikes the tinder, it begins to glow.

We can tell what's happening from our reaction. Suppose something malicious is done. Some people have very unselfishly done a great service and built something up.

Then somebody comes along and, for no reason at all, breaks it down and destroys it. When that happens to someone else, I think, 'Oh, deplorable! So sad!' And then I go all psychological and say, 'Of course, you know, the *real* sufferer is the man who has done this mindlessly spiteful thing — he's the *real* sufferer.' But if it happens to me, then it's quite different. Now that's a tinder situation, when it happens to me. What I've built up unselfishly and not for personal gratification, glory or power, is wantonly kicked to pieces, out of sheer devilment.

It is one of the cases that's given in Zen.

The teacher says to a man to whom this has happened, 'What is your feeling now?'

The man struggles with himself and says, 'Well, I suppose I'm telling myself, "That poor fellow, he's making very bad karma for himself, and I'm sorry for him."'

Now the teacher says, 'No good at all!'

'What?'

'That's no good at all. You've got to drink him down to the last drop of poison.'

When the teacher says something like that to me, I think: 'U - u - gh!'

And then the teacher says (and this is in one of the old Zen books), 'You've got to drink him down to the last drop of venom.

'Let the bird fly in the vast sky of your
    serenity:
Set the fish free in the bottomless ocean
    of your tolerance.

'Do that. Love has to be brave enough to drink up the person entirely, poison and all.'

And I think, 'Oh, you can't expect me to do that.'

Well, that's the tinder. If that spark strikes, then there's a chance, just a chance, if it's preserved, that my attitude can change and I can move out of that cycle of grudging acceptance into something different.

And then I say, 'Well, what am I supposed to do? Supposing I do drink him down. Am I just to let it go, encourage him to do it again?'

The teacher says, 'No! The words of love are not necessarily only kindly words.'

On this point I thought I'd give one or two short examples from my own experience as a judo practitioner (at which I've spent a good many years) and as a teacher (at which I've also spent a good many years). Now I've retired, I've hardly been to the judo halls for perhaps twenty years, because young people, some of them my pupils, are teachers now. But very occasionally I have to go and I went on one anniversary. The teacher there is a very good man; he's been an English champion, and he's a very good teacher.

He said to me, 'There's a young fellow here, he's desperately keen. He's got a very poor physique, but he's trying like mad. Would you have a word with him?'

'No, I don't want to. He's your pupil, you teach him.' I remembered when I was young how these old boys used to totter up. 'No, I don't want to do that.'

'He must see you. You've got to, you've got to.'

So I saw this kid. Well, when you get old you get sort of kindly and so on; and it's all so terrible really that you can't say it's good or bad. So I saw this young chap trying his stuff.

'It's very good, yes, very good, bravo!'

So he bowed and went off. Afterwards the teacher came to me. He said, 'You know, he was terribly disappointed with what you said.'

'Oh?'

'He expected you to say something. He wants to get on. Please see him again.'

So I saw him again and I told him, 'You're no good and you'll be no good for three years; and you've only got one chance in a hundred of achieving what you want to achieve. But if you do this and this and this, and you build up to two hundred repetitions every day, and you practise like mad, you've got one chance in a hundred.'

Well, he had asked for it and he got it. Some years later I was pleased to know that he'd won the junior championship of Britain. Words of love are not necessarily kindly words, and words which are kindly, are not necessarily to the benefit of the person.

We're told in one of the schools that the

things that happen in training are like a vaccination. You get a little bit of the illness under controlled conditions and then your body can learn how to throw if off. Later on, if you're exposed to a big infection, your body can throw it off easily. In the same way, some of the things which happen in training are designed so that we have a little experience and we learn how to meet that experience; later on, when life throws something on the same lines but much bigger at us, we shall know the method.

There was a Master called Iida, some of whose books are difficult to read; they're old books from the beginning of the century. I've been over parts of one with a good Zen teacher who's also an excellent scholar and he told me, 'In places, I don't know what the old boy meant. He just throws difficult Chinese texts at you.' But in one section he lists in an illuminating way some of what a former Master, Gudō, calls Zen illnesses.

The first one is: Lack of Faith, that your faith doesn't go far enough. He says, 'It's not so much faith in what will be, as faith in what is. We have to have faith in what is now. We all know what people say they think — it comes out in their words; but often those same words also give away the true state of affairs.'

If you've done judo, you're sometimes asked to control people who are drunk. And anybody who's ever had to do that is very familiar with the phrase, 'I'm not so think as you drunk I am.' We know what he means, but the very way he says it tells us the opposite.

Iida says, 'The heart of faith.' This is a phrase also used by Rinzai. What is the heart of faith? He says, 'The one who asks is the heart.' And what is faith? 'The fact that he asks is faith. Now, if he can isolate those two in himself — what is it that's asking, and what is this asking — then he'll come to the heart of faith. It's not a matter of words.'

Perfection is often represented by a great circle. A man tried with Master Takuan. He made with his finger a big circle in the air, and said, 'The Buddha, Buddha-nature — it's a great circle, means perfection.' He was in an exalted state as he said it.

And the teacher said, 'What?'

'Buddha-nature — perfection! Perfect circle!'

'Eh?'

'THE BUDDHA-NATURE IS PERFECTION! CIRCLE!'

'There's an angle here somewhere.'

Iida, this Zen Master from whom I've taken some of the illustrations, sometimes turns the phrases round on their heads, but it makes us think about them and it can be a stimulus. There's a saying that the karma must ripen and the season must come, and the person who's been loyally practising — then he gets it! But Iida says, 'The karma and the season came long ago; *they're* waiting for *you*! It's the persons who are lacking.'

Faith in the Universe. The example given is growing roses. He says, 'The gardener can't actually get inside the rose and go uhh! uhh! uhh! uhh! He has to have faith in the rose; then he removes obstacles. If there's a lack of water, he supplies it. But when you say that the gardener grows roses, this is only in a secondary use of the term. The roses grow; the gardener removes the obstructions.'

Another example from gardening, of which I may say I know nothing, but this example is always given. (And I have the feeling sometimes that it's given by people who also don't know much about gardening.) One's told, 'Don't look for results. Think of tiny children; when you were a little child you planted seeds and the next day, "Oh!, nothing's come up." And the next day you thought, "I'll dig them up and see what's going on." How ridiculous, isn't it!' But an experienced gardener says, 'Yes, of course, that's ridiculous to dig them up after two days. On the other hand, if you put down the seeds six years ago, and you left them alone, and you walked over them and maybe even put rubbish on top of them and *then* nothing happened, it might be time to do a bit of digging up and plant some fresh seeds!'

The next illness is: Acquiring Things. Here's an example, not from Iida, but what I heard quite some years back from a Zen preacher. One of the most popular film stars in Japan is, or was then, Alain Delon. The preacher was instancing a Japanese husband and wife. He said, 'The husband's working hard, getting on, and the wife's doing well; she's bringing up the child. But one day she spends the afternoon, instead of doing the household chores, looking at a television picture of Alain Delon. And she's very taken with this. Then shortly before her husband comes back, she puts on the apron so that he'll think, "What a hard-working wife I've got," and busily gets everything ready. Then he comes in and she looks at him and thinks, "Why aren't you more like Alain Delon?" But as a matter of fact, in the train on the way back, *he's* been reading a magazine about Alain Delon, and he looks at her and he thinks, "Why aren't you more like the glamorous women that Alain Delon comes back to?"' And that preacher said, 'Now, they've both got something in their minds; they've acquired something, and that spoils their life, momentarily.' Then he made the further point that it's something that doesn't exist, because what they've seen on the film is a creation of make-up and lights and camera angles.

And the actual film stars, when you meet them, are nothing at all like what they are on the screen. So they've put something which is already illusory into their minds, and they have it at the back of their minds when they're talking to each other. Now, this is the great illness of acquiring something — putting something into your mind which doesn't exist.

The next illness is: No Persistence. Iida explains how people start with a tremendous burst of enthusiasm (Nirvana now and beat the rush!), but they can't keep it up; they don't keep it up. Then he mentions quite an interesting point about tricks. I recognize this from judo. You can teach people in their first year certain things which will get quick results; they're surprising tricks and they'll get very quick results in the contests in the first year.

I knew a pair of brothers who were not from any *dōjō* where I've taught, whose teacher had taught them three or four of these tricks. They must have spent a lot of time on them. When they came up to one of the central clubs for the grading contest, they sometimes won in two or three seconds. It was most dramatic — marvellous! like a miracle, like a magic trick . . . man goes over — bang! And very pleasant for the examiners too.

But these things have an inherent limit: the effect is mainly from surprise. After a year, they've got the brown belt (this is one below the famous black belt). But other Brown Belts have been around; they've seen most of what there is to be seen and these tricks now no longer work, they won't get any results at all against Brown Belts. A man who's spent his time acquiring them, doesn't have throws which can develop; he's only got tricks which now no longer work because they depended on surprise. And those two brothers, although they shot ahead in their first year, were stuck for three years and couldn't advance any further, while the people whom they'd beaten so brilliantly in the early stages went ahead of them.

This, in the spiritual traditions, is called 'sneaking in by the side door'. There are, so to speak, tricks by which people can have immediate results which seem to be very impressive, especially to themselves. But these things have inherent limitations; they can't progress further, they can't lead to anything. People who sneak in through the side door without an invitation, not coming in through the front door, soon get discovered and, as the teacher says, they get thrown out.

The successes, these dramatic successes which can be attained by tricks, are generally disastrous. Without saying anything about Buddhism, in judo you never improve from success; you nearly always get worse because your head gets bigger and bigger when you've had a success. Then you think,

'Oh, no need to study any more.' Whereas when you have a failure, then you analyse and make progress. So, 'The early successes', he says, 'in Zen, are not very favourable, because what seem to be early successes, what the man himself thinks are early successes, affect his persistence.'

Then the next illness is said to be a very very serious illness indeed and this is: to Hang On to one's Own Ideas, to hang on with a clenched fist to one's own ideas. One can use a good deal of resources if one is ingenious, to protect and develop one's own ideas; the intellect can be used.

You say to the intellect, 'Look, this training's getting boring. Get me out of this.'

And intellect says, 'Well, of course, I speak as an outsider. I can only bring in pure reason, but it seems to me — correct me if I'm wrong — Buddhism is supposed to remove the ego, is it not?'

'Yes.'

'Well now, if you're saying, "*I'm* going to practise; *I'm* going to keep up this discipline", well, that's an assertion of the ego; you're strengthening the very thing you're supposed to be weakening!'

Intellect, as a sort of devil in a frockcoat, speaks from the point of view of reason — it sounds all right. Then — with luck — one of the little imps who is aping his master, shouts enthusiastically, 'Yes, that's right, and don't make your breakfast either because you'll be thinking, "*I* am making breakfast," and that will impair your spiritual practice too.' The hollowness of the whole argument is now exposed. If we're going to do anything, then we should do the spiritual practice.

Iida gives this example: A man with a bitter tongue went to his teacher and said, 'Nirvana is here now. Why do spiritual practice?'

And the teacher said, 'Yes, Nirvana is here now. Why go round slandering people?' He had that bitter tongue.

If spiritual practice is not to be done because it's not necessary, then by the same reasoning, our ordinary activities also should not be done. If I'm not to do spiritual practice because it'll increase my egotism, then I shouldn't make the breakfast because that'll increase my egotism.

We have to be trained and we don't know the training that we need, because the training we need will be directed at our weak point. The training I'd like to do would be the training of my strong point where I can show off like mad. Suppose that at judo I'm very strong on the right; I can get results on the right; I can throw people on the right. Suddenly the teacher says, 'You've got to give up the right for six months and only use the left.' Well, then I look a fool; I can't throw people with the left; it's ridiculous. I can do things this way; I can't do things that way. Why does he insist I should do it that way? They all say, 'Old Leggett's going off, you know. Can't throw anyone.' Well, it takes considerable effort to get over that and to think, 'All right, I'm going to look a fool for six months.' Then both the sides balance and as a matter of fact when the left is developed, the right too becomes stronger. If the right is developed by itself and the left side is undeveloped, even that apparent strength of the right is defective.

We're trained in what we need. As a Japanese Zen teacher told me, 'Don't think that Zen came to Japan because it suits the Japanese people. No, Zen came to Japan because it's what the Japanese people need.'

Among the judo fraternity, the roughest are the medical students. I practised once with such a man. (I didn't know where he came from.) Normally in the *dōjō*, the practice hall, people just come up and say, '*O-negai*', 'Will you?' This chap came up and made a very deep formal bow; '*O-negai-itashimasu*', 'May I have the honour of practising with you?'

'Oh, all right.'

He was like a typhoon — all elbows and knees and hacks. When first he threw me, as I was getting off the floor, he drew himself up and said, 'Please excuse me.'

I thought, 'Whew, what's this?'

Then, when I threw him, same thing; he got up off the floor, stood straight, bowed and said, 'Thank you very much.' And then it was all elbows, knees and hacks again.

I realized later that the teacher in the medical judo *dōjō* knew that was what they needed. He made them have very strict politeness so that it would calm them down, restrain them a little bit, just for a moment in the middle of the excitement. It would restrain them and hold them to something formal and peaceful, honouring and respecting the opponent. He knew they would be liable to lose their tempers, so that was imposed.

One judo man I knew was the opposite. He was a marvellously skilful man, but he was too kind-hearted. He used to think, 'If I beat this chap, he'll be all depressed and sorry.' And you'd say, 'Look, he's come here to try; he's come here to fail; he wants you to go all out.' But whatever you said it didn't make any difference, he was too nice, he was too kind. Well, just before one big contest, the teacher called him out of the hall, round into a corner, and said, 'I've just got something to tell you before the contest.' And the teacher spat in his face. It's a nasty experience. The teacher wiped it off and said, 'Now go on, get back.' To all our amazement this man who usually went up very very politely and considerately to the platform, was striding along with his face like iron. And he won in no time. Well, that was his, not exactly weak point, but he was too nice and it was against the spirit of contest, which is to fight very very hard and then afterwards to be very good friends. The whole basis is peace, but on that peace, for the sake of sport, there's this intense competition and rivalry. The personal ideas have to be given up, we have to accept that the training will be to our weak point.

Now Iida says, 'The students must understand that their meditation and spiritual practice must spread out from the meditation period into their ordinary activities.' To merely follow instructions — that's not enough.

We never do these things, or hardly ever do these things now, but I had a certain experience of it when a teacher offered to show me something special. So I stood there and he said, 'Now you cross the wrist over here.' So I crossed the wrist over there, and as I was doing it, he slapped me on the face.

'Wha . . what?'

'You can't just do that. You're a judo man; you're supposed to be awake; you're not supposed to be just crossing a wrist and not paying attention to what I might do. I'm here!' Then he told me to cross the wrists again, but this time I was alert, not mechanically thinking, 'Oh well, I'll just do this. This is what's wanted, I'll do it.' No — total awareness.

In the same way, when spiritual practice is done, the whole life must be alert to it; it's not just a question of doing one thing at one time and place.

The next illness is: Failure to Mature.
People practise and get what he calls a
little bit of fire in them, but it doesn't mature. They're satisfied and they think, 'I've
got something,' and they go off and it
doesn't mature. But one of the problems, as
we know, is that you're told, 'Of course it
takes a long, long time — twenty years
under the hammer, thirty years under the
hammer (and you begin to wait for the auc-
tioneer to say, "forty years under the hammer", don't you?), before you'll get anything.'
One example is this. I knew a retired
schoolmaster who was marvellous at chess
problems. He sometimes used to win the
national competition that they held at the
time. He used to set up the position in his
house on a board. When he was walking
about, he'd look at it for a few minutes and
try one or two moves, write down the result
that he'd got, then pass on. He was getting
on in years so he couldn't concentrate for
hours on it. I said to him, 'How long does it
take?' He said, 'I reckon it'll take about
two days; then I'll have the solution. We're
given a week.' Now, if each time he'd
looked at it he'd thought, 'Oh well, it's
going to take two days,' he would never
have solved it. Each time he looked at it,
he had to think, 'Now! now! try this one!
now!' And his experience was that generally it would be wrong — but it might be
right. And therefore, Iida says, 'Because

you're told that it will take some time
maturing, don't think, "Oh well, here we go
trudging along."   No.   Think: "Now! Now!
Now!"'

One of the applications is this.   In this
country we tend to think that you can't
really get results unless you are directly
driven by some passion.   People say, 'You
won't win unless you've got the killer instinct — nice people don't win!'   Well, it's
quite true that people who have the killer
instinct often do win, but if you've ever
seen in a competitive antagonistic situation
— someone who's lost his temper, up against
a good technician who manages to keep his
head — well then you've seen an absolute
massacre, because 'desire has no eyes' (this
is one of the Zen sayings which Iida quotes),
and 'temper can't wait'.

In one of Shaw's plays, *How He Lied to
Her Husband*, the poet is in love with the
wife of a big man who's got a furious temper.   They hear him coming back.   They
hear him clumping about downstairs.   And
she says, 'He'll kill you!'

The poet says, 'Oh no, I'm a poet, you
know, and like all poets, I go in for boxing.
It's true I'm a lightweight; I'm a lightweight,
but I'm quite agile enough to keep out of
your husband's way until his temper gets him
all puffed, and after that I shall be all over
him.'

'What do you mean by "all over him?"'
'Best not ask, dear.'

The killer instinct, the temper, the fury: it does get results, but there is something higher. One of the analogies that's given is the yacht. Many people think that the yacht goes fastest when the wind is directly behind blowing it forward, but the yacht can go faster if it's across the wind. The mechanical principle involved is different — the inclined plane — and the yacht can go faster than the wind. Most people find this incredible, but it can be looked up and verified. There has to be a keel to hold the boat steady. This example is given in Zen. The passions are not directly opposed, but they're crossed and so made use of in a spiritual way. The heart-yacht doesn't run directly before the passions; it runs across them.

In the application of the spiritual principles, as in the judo techniques, they must work. Iida makes quite a point of this. He says, 'Things may be very beautiful; things may be very appealing; things may be very touching, very kindly, but unless they work, they're not Zen.' And perhaps we see this today. There is great kindliness with your Welfare State, but it's what Confucius used to call sentimentality — benevolence without wisdom. Something's gone wrong. Iida stresses, 'It must work.' And in judo I can remember a beautiful stylist. He said to me once, 'You know, as I pick myself off the floor, they say, "Oh, but you've got such a lovely style."'

Now, Iida further says, we have to find enlightenment in each instant. We all know this experience: we go to a beautiful place in the country and we think, 'Oh, this'll be heaven.' After three or four days, 'Oh no, no, it gets humpy, you know, nothing doing.'

A modern Zen teacher shouted at his audience: 'Hakuin's "Song of Meditation" says, "The place where you are, that is the Lotus Paradise." You're in air-polluted Tokyo, so don't complain: Tokyo is your Lotus Paradise.'

We have to find these things in ourselves, in the ordinary movements. If we look at children we see they've got a joy in movement. The baby on the lawn this afternoon, he sees this coloured ball going along. He kicks it and he's laughing: the yellow moving on the green. He's getting pleasure out of running. Well, we watch dully and we think, 'Oh just a ball . . .' What's gone wrong? What have we lost? We had these things. Now Iida tells us, 'There's something which we're missing.'

This room — suppose we are asked to describe everything in it and we do. Then they say, 'No, you've left something out.' We describe more detail. 'No, you've left something out.' Every tiny detail. 'No, you've left something out.' Now what is it? Light! Nobody ever describes light. We don't say, 'Oh, we're seeing light.' And yet everything we see is light. An artist does; he's the only person who describes the light.

But all that we see is light. In the same way, there's stillness and movement, and there's a joy in these two things, but we don't think of that; we don't feel a joy in movement. All we think is, 'I've got to do this and that next.' Babies feel it. So Iida tells us, 'There's something in our ordinary experience which we miss and which we must recover.'

Well, the last thing Iida says is, 'If you talk too much, the universe begins to yawn!' So I will shut up.

FINGERS AND MOONS

FINGERS AND MOONS

This isn't a formal lecture at all; it's just like a few pebbles thrown at a window to wake up someone who's sleeping inside. If the sleeper doesn't wake up, then throw some more. So it's in the hope that one or two will wake one or two people up, temporarily at least, as some of them have woken me up, temporarily at least, that I pass on some of them. It's called *Fingers and Moons*, and this relates to a phrase 'The finger pointing to the moon'. This is generally illustrated by a finger pointing to a full moon which everyone can see. It's rather pointless. But really the saying arose from trying to see the new moon. As an example: There was a fasting austerity in India called 'The ant body'. An ant's body, as you know, begins big and comes down very thin and then gets bigger again. So in this austerity, you started on the full moon day with fourteen mouthfuls of food and water and then each day you reduced it by one mouthful; when it got to the dark night you had nothing. Then, when the new moon appeared, you could have your first, only one, mouthful of water or food.   And you gradually increased it until you got up to fourteen mouthfuls a day.   It's not much, if you've ever tried it.   Seeing the new moon, then, was quite important, and it can be difficult to make out the little thread.

The Chinese saying is: 'With a deaf man, you show the gate by pointing with your finger; with a blind man, you show the gate by knocking on it.' They're different means, and the plural 'fingers' implies that there are different means of getting one to see. If we think, 'Oh! there *is* only one means', then we may be restricting our view. Still, as a rule it's best to practise just one of the means.

Another thing is this.   It's worth experimenting, pointing your finger at the moon one night and seeing what actually happens. People can write a book on fingers pointing to the moon and it's quite clear they've never tried it.   What actually happens is (if your sight is normal), you point the finger towards the moon and focus on the finger. The finger is clear, but you will see two vague moons beyond it; they're not at all clear.   The finger is brilliantly clear.   Then you make a sort of leap; you change the focus to the moon.   Now you will see the moon brilliantly clear, but you will see two transparent fingers.

It's worth trying this as an illustration of our practice. These illustrations are not given for nothing and sometimes they're very precise as to the details. When we're following a pointing finger, the pointing finger can become very very clear, but the goal very vague. When the time comes, we have to take a leap beyond that very clear finger to the goal; it's a change of focus, not of direction. And then the means we were using become almost transparent — the moon becomes clear.

There are people who say with considerable pride, 'I don't want fingers or methods. I want to see the moon *directly! directly! . .* to see the moon *directly!* — no methods or pointing.' But in fact they don't see it. It's easy to say.

There are others who can be lost in the finger. You can study the finger; you can put rings on it; but you forget what its purpose was. The forms are the methods and they're very important as a pointing finger, but if we forget what they're for and they become, so to speak, the goal in their own right, then our progress is liable to stop, and because it stops it will retrogress.

One Zen teacher talks about the reverence to a priest. Would you give that same reverence if he was a well-known swindler, a seller of fake charms? If you think it obligatory, even when you know, and he knows you

know, that the situation is false and that
your bow is not a genuine reverence, what's
the situation?   In Western history it would
be the situation of a particular philosopher
who was arrested and punished for not ap-
plauding Nero's verses sufficiently enthusiastically — he failed to clap loud enough at
the Emperor's verses.   This was a completely false situation into which Nero's
subjects were driven.

As an example of form and reverence,
at one of the great temples there is a lineage from the present abbot right back to
the Buddha.   The tradition of the sect is
that the lineage must be read before the
altar every day at the service.   There are
something over one hundred names on that
lineage now and each name has to be ac-
companied with a particular form of reverential salutation, so that if you really read
them like that, it would take a long time.
Well, people haven't got the time for this
now — but the names *must* be read.   So they
divide the list up into four parts, twenty-
five names on each; and then four priests
come together in front of the altar and read
the four lists simultaneously.   The names are
read, the tradition is preserved; it sounds
odd, but at least the service gets a move on.

It's very easy to follow forms and feel
one gets support from the forms.   The forms
support each other, too: I may not feel very
reverential, but when I see the other people
bowing so reverentially, then I feel supported

and encouraged to do it myself. But supposing they feel the same way? They are relying on me. Hakuin compares this to trees whose branches interlace. You get a whole wood of them. Now they're holding each other up. And even when the roots are withering, the trees still stand up. It's like a table with many legs. There's no depth of root at all, and the trees don't put out much in the way of green, or fruit, or flower, but they hold each other up. One day a storm comes and everything goes down. When the wind blows, an individual tree can only remain up by depending on his neighbours, and *they* can only remain up depending on others. So, if one is blown, there's a strain on the whole community. But in a healthy growth, as Hakuin says, 'When each tree has strong individual roots, then they protect each other. The trees on the north side have their own roots; they can stand up. When the north wind comes, they protect the others; they're not leaning on the others; they're standing by their own roots and they protect the others. And when the wind comes from the south they, in turn, are protected by the others — but the trees have their *own* roots.' And he uses this illustration to show that when the forms begin to get more and more elaborate, more and more magnificent, and more and more *apparently* reverential, it can be just interlaced trees holding each other up.

On the subject of the tree, the Chinese character for a tree shows the root:

If *we're* asked to draw a tree, we just draw the trunk and the foliage — that's a tree! But to the Chinese, that's not a whole tree at all; there's at least as much below the ground as there is above the ground. And that which is below the ground is as important, or more important, than what's above the ground — that makes up the whole tree.

Now, one of the illustrations given, which is quite an important one for people who are doing practice, is of the cherry tree. The cherry tree flowers just for two or three weeks once a year. The Japanese cherry doesn't have fruit or much in the way of fragrance, but it blossoms very beautifully. The blossoms don't rot on the branch. When they're still in their fulness, they fall. This is said to be like a man of the true spiritual way: In the fulness, he can easily leave the branch without any regrets or hanging on past the time.

People turn up in hundreds of thousands to see the cherry blossoms and they hang poems on the trees, even now. Many of the people, the ordinary people, can write poems and they hang them on the trees. They come to appreciate these cherry blossoms. In front of my London house, too, there are three streets with Japanese cherries, and if you go out when the moon is nearly full, shining on the white cherry blossoms — it's a sight that you never forget. This happens once a year. The illustration given is this. People see that wonderful flowering; then, at other times of the year, the cherries are not flowering. So they think somehow the cherries are failing. But this isn't so. There are three weeks of blossoming and forty-nine weeks when the roots are going deeper, when, as the Chinese phrase goes, 'the thunder enters the earth' — the vitality goes right down into the roots. That, and

the period of the blossoming, form a unity.
It's not that the cherry's depressed and sad
and failing, and then suddenly it has a wonderful success; and then that success, alas,
is all too passing, taken away. No! — it's a
single tree. What to the human being is the
moment of glory, and that other time when
the vitality is in the roots — they form a
unity.

I can give one example from judo. An
experienced teacher can look at the build of
keen young students — the limbs all differ
and the proportions differ — but sometimes
one has an exceptional facility with one
particular movement. He can see that this
could develop into a particular throw which
is rather difficult to do. He says to him,
'Now look, if you practise this throw,'
(which he shows him) 'if you practise it a
hundred thousand times, by then you will
have got the knack. There's a sort of knack
which can't be imitated or taught, but it can
only be felt, you'll get the knack.'

Now he practises, and he fails and fails.
It takes some time, but if you think of a
hundred thousand, apart from his ordinary
competitive practice, a keen student might
do, say, a hundred a day. In a year that
would be thirty thousand, assuming he practised six days a week, as most of them do,
if not seven. In three years he could have
got through a hundred thousand — then, he
will have got the knack. But it would be
quite wrong for him after, say, one year to

think, 'Oh well, of course, I've still got two years to go. I can't get it now.' No! he may get it any time. What the teacher is telling him is that it may take a hundred thousand repetitions, and often does, to get that knack. But the student doesn't think that, he thinks, 'Today! today! today!' when he tries. He thinks, 'Now! now! now!' as he tries his daily hundred.

Well, this is also a hint for spiritual practice. People are told, 'It will take a long time.' It does take a long time in many cases, but it doesn't follow that there's got to be a particular length of time. The awareness is there and can be realized now, now, now!

One further development which you might find a parallel to, when a promising young judo man is told this by a really experienced teacher — this is faith. The teacher has faith *in him*. People don't realize that; they think, 'Oh, faith is a question for the pupil.' No, the teacher has faith that he'll be able to do this. Otherwise he wouldn't teach it to him. A pupil does it for about six months, and he fails and he fails and he fails. Now, from the teacher's point of view, the hundred thousand failures and the one success form a unity. So they're not failures; they form a unity — the hundred thousand movements and the one success — just like the cherry trees. It's not that the cherry tree's failing and failing and failing to put out flowers: it forms a unity — the roots are going deeper, and then the flowers will come out.

After six months that young judo man will meet what in judo circles are referred to by various uncomplimentary names, the most acceptable being 'the old soldiers'. One of them says, 'Look, I've been here fourteen years.' (His grade is not very high, but he's quite impressive with his reminiscences of the past.) He goes on, 'You know, they don't expect you to do this. They tell you this because it'll get you to do something, you see, but they don't really expect you to bring off that throw after a hundred thousand or a hundred million repetitions; you can't do it unless you've been born in Japan and are brought up there and so on. You can't do that, no, but keep on trying, you know, you'll get a bit better. But don't expect that you're ever going to pull it off.'

Well now, when somebody's about eighteen and he's told that by an old boy who's been there, seen it all, you know, come in the back door, the front door, the side door, knows it all, he begins to hesitate. He begins to think, 'I wonder if that's right. Do they tell everybody this? Do they just tell you, "Well, after a hundred thousand at most you'll have it?"'

A young teacher, when he sees this, tends to get uneasy and thinks, 'He's being talked out of this.' So he generally goes to a very senior teacher and says, 'Look, this is what's happening. That old . . . , he's talking him out of it. Do you think I ought to have another word with him and just sort of . . .' And the old teacher replies, 'No! Now, look at you. You were in the British team at your peak and since then, as a teacher, you've produced some good men. You've written a couple of books on judo — one of them was quite good — and you're fairly well know. Now, he's your pupil and you've told him this. He's either going to believe you, or he's going to believe that no-good who's never done anything himself and doesn't want anyone else to do anything either. It's a question of faith.' So the old teacher says, 'Leave him. Either he'll have the faith — he'll keep on with it, and then he'll confirm it, and then he'll trust you ever afterwards — or he won't. But if you have to keep pushing him, then next time you'll have to push him again, and next time you'll have to push him again. Now's the time he can develop faith. You've got faith in him: let him have faith in you.'

We teach these special techniques which people can acquire. After perhaps eight years a man who's very keen and has a good teacher, can get an extraordinary skill in one or two moves. He then identifies himself with that skill that he's got, and when he comes up to a contest he thinks, 'This is how I'm going to win — by this special technique I've developed.' Of course, a first aim is usually to find out what special

technique the other man has developed, so
that one can guard against it. Well, you
generally get confusing and conflicting re-
ports about a prospective opponent. Some
people tell you, 'Oh, he's like a bomb at the
beginning, but if you can survive that, he's
got nothing. He's just got this one terrific
throw.' And then somebody says, 'Oh no!
he's given that up; he's given that up
altogether! He hangs on now till the fourth
minute, *then* he explodes.' After you've had
a certain amount of experience, you wipe all
that aside, 'I'll just fight the man as he is.'

But for ourselves, we build up a special
excellence and we think we'll fight with
that, and we can win with that — but
there's a limit. The special excellence is
something that's, so to speak, like a block of
ice; it can't go through a sieve. As the
grade goes up and up, opponents can put up
the bars against these special excellences
when they get to know of them. Now he
has to throw away that special skill and take
the small and tiny opportunities as they
occur. It's very difficult to do this, just as
it's very difficult to give up one's particular
technique which one's good at for handling
life.

People come to the judo hall and they
say, 'Look, I'm not very good at judo, but I
am good at accounts and organizing. I'll
take over all the accounts and the organizing — do it for nothing. You'll all be free
to practise.' Well, that's a very bad thing

for a judo *dōjō*. Another man, he's a skilled carpenter; he's terrified of judo, but he wants to be associated with it, so he says, 'I'll do all the repairs.' And you have new benches and you have new racks in the changing room and it's all sort of transformed. The members are doing nothing towards it, and that's very bad. And you get another man: he'll sweep out the showers and the lavatory and do it beautifully; they are spotless, but he's not doing much judo practice. That's bad for him and it's bad for the judo enthusiasts. So in a judo club we always prevent this happening, and the team members, however good and skilful they may be, are on their knees scrubbing out the showers along with the others. This makes a great difference to the whole atmosphere of the place; it brings a unity into it.

In our Western sports, and in a good many other things too, the tigers won't play with the rabbits. In the Budo (knightly arts including judo), however much of a tiger a man is — he's in the club team, perhaps in the county team, perhaps in the national team, and he practises like mad — he always gives twenty minutes of his time every day to giving some instruction to a beginner, to a complete beginner, in order to bring this unity — not that some are sort of performing stars and the others are just watching them, but so that there's a unity.

We can imitate things; we can imitate

pointing fingers; we can imitate spiritual attitudes which are supposed to lead to progress. But those imitations don't lead to anything — they're like putting rings on the fingers. The pointing finger should be studied carefully, but if it becomes an end in itself, then the practice will drop. As an example there is an Indian story, a Hindu story, but it contains rather a good lesson. There were two brothers who used to worship every day. One used to use many vessels of gold and silver to do this ceremony — very elaborately — (there are such ceremonies in Buddhism too) and it used to take him about an hour. He did it with great devotion and sincerity; everything was precise, absolutely accurate, and he did all the prayers. Now his brother never did anything like that; he didn't even have a fixed time for praying, but when he felt the impulse, he would stand and clasp his hands for a few minutes, then go about his business. Well, the ceremonialist, as you might call him, had an impulse to find out what happened to their prayers, or anyway his prayers. He was told of a ceremony which would give the vision and he did it. He has the vision of a great courtyard full of flowers, and attendants are loading these flowers onto carts. A voice tells him, 'These carts are bound for the halls of the Most High. And these flowers are the prayers of the two brothers.' The place is full of flowers. Then he looks round and he sees a little posy, and he realizes that this is the prayers of his brother. And it looks rather pathetic. But when he looks carefully he sees it's got a beauty of its own, a simple beauty of its own.

Then one of the attendants calls out to the others, 'Quick! hasten, hasten! We must get these flowers cleared away and sent to the halls before the next lot arrive.'

The ceremonial brother feels sorry for them and steps forward and says, 'Well, there's no need to hurry because I shall not be praying until this evening.'

The attendant replies, 'Oh, we can handle any number of those little posies, but your brother is about to pray again and the whole place will be deluged with flowers!'

That man had a technique of prayer. It was not bad — can't say it was a bad thing — but there was something much higher. In all the arts and in life generally, we get a technique of handling things. Our technique might be helplessness, 'Oh, I could never mend a fuse. No, I've never been any good at that,' and people rush to mend it and I say, 'Oh aren't they clever.' That can be a technique, an effective one. I might use it very successfully. But if I'm alone and the fuse goes, I'll find I can get up and mend it quite well. Some people have other techniques: 'I look at everything scientifically.' 'I look at everything, well, historically.' 'I look at everything from the point of view of kindness — got to be kind to people. If a

man says he's thirsty, give him a drink; if
he's still thirsty, give him another drink.'
(If he's undiagnosed diabetic you'll be killing
him, but that doesn't matter; it's 'kind'.
Confucius said that benevolence without
wisdom is only sentimentality and doesn't
lead to much.)

Our technique, then, has to be given up.
We think, 'What!?' In judo, when the
teacher tells us (and he says this only to
people who are determined to improve),
'You've mastered that. Now give it up for
at least six months,' we think, 'What? I'm
not allowed to do that? I go on the mat and
I'm not allowed to use my big throw. I've
got to try other things that I can't do — I
get countered, I look an absolute fool!'
Now many of us fail that test. We think,
'Oh no, no! I'm not going to do this,' and
we go back to what we can do, and we get
some successes. But those who've got faith
in the teacher and who realize that the
teacher's got faith in them, they persist and
then they begin to develop a free movement,
not fixed on one point — they can move
freely. If the opportunity's here, they can
take it; if it's there, they can take it —
they're not fixed.

There are supposed to be people who
prepare jokes. I think it was the American
poet Ogden Nash who wrote a story about a
man who thought, 'Well, there's a proverb,
isn't there, "The shoemaker should stick to
his last." I'm going to this big party, and

there will probably be a man there called
Schumacher (a common name in America)
and very likely he'll have been divorced, but
he won't be getting on very well with his
new wife. And then I shall say to him,
"Schumacher, you should have stuck to your
last!"' And it describes this man going
round the party trying to find a divorced
Schumacher who's having trouble with his
new wife — but he never finds one. Well,
it's a bit like that when we have our favour-
ite techniques in life. We go round looking
for opportunities, trying to manoeuvre
opportunities, so that we can bring off the
big gun. But actually people somehow get a
sort of instinct for not getting in front of a
big gun, even though it may be hidden in the
bushes.

These methods fail in the end, so we
have to give them up. In judo it's called
'cutting off the bull's horns'. After eight
years' intense practice, you develop something very strong and that's the bull's horns
— that's what you fight with. Now you're
asked to cut them off. And that means one
becomes a beginner again. This is a very
important part of the spiritual side as well
as the technical side of judo training. The
teachers also tell us, and they put it into
practice too, that when we're becoming
strong and well known, and when we've mastered something, then we should take up
something else where we're going to be no
good at all. If you're a violinist, and you've

mastered the violin, then take up the piano and you'll be stumbling over five-finger exercises. They say, 'When you've become a great big frog in your own pond and you're puffing yourself up, go into the neighbouring pond and become a tadpole, a tiny little tadpole.' And this is again, cutting off and being able to go freely into those other forms.

There's a poem which applies to these fixed successful attitudes in life and it's used in all the training schools in Japan. There's a particular mountain where the trees and the bushes are, or were, so thick that nothing could get through at all. The poem is this:

> *The trees on Mount Ibuka*
> *Are not so thick*
> *That from time to time*
> *A ray of moonlight*
> *Cannot pierce through the branches.*

Nothing solid can come through, but a ray of clear awareness can come through. All our cultivated habits of thought and will fail in certain circumstances, but clear awareness is able to penetrate through any obstacle.

Buddha-nature, where is it? It doesn't seem to be anywhere. The teacher says, 'But it's here . . .' It's something which we know we haven't got, and yet we have. One method of teaching this is through history. It's no use citing examples from Chinese or

Japanese history which take long explanations, so I'll give one or two examples
from our history. All of you can read
silently. You can pick up a letter and you
can read it. But in the Middle Ages and in
classical times, they couldn't do that. They
had to verbalize; they had to speak it aloud
before they could understand — that was the
only way they could read.

This was true of Japan too. A Russian
captain in the eighteenth century, who was
wrecked on the coast, was held in prison for
a time till the authorities could investigate
him. He complained to the guard that he
was keeping him awake at night by reading
aloud. He said, 'Please read quietly.' 'But,'
the guard said, 'this is the only way I can
read. Unless I say the words, I can't read.'

St. Augustine could read silently and he
was regarded as a great, an unparalleled,
genius because he could do this. But everybody here can do it. Are we all unparalleled
geniuses? Perhaps we are, but certainly at
that time they couldn't find this capacity in
themselves.

The mediavel people built great ca-
thedrals; these were tremendous triumphs of
organization, and the finances were pretty
complicated too. But the accountants
couldn't multiply in the head more than five
times five. No human being could remember
the tables after that! So they had them
posted up on the walls. And if the accountant was away from his posted-up tables and

he wanted to multiply, say, seven times seven — well, naturally, one can't remember things like that. He would hold up a hand and put down the fingers above five. Seven — so you put two down and leave three up. The same with the other hand. Then you add the fingers that are down — four — (they are the tens) and you multiply the fingers that are up (three times three) — nine — and you've got the answer — forty-nine. Professional accountants used this method. There are references in the literature of the time to 'the supple fingers of accountants', because they were doing this all the time. We can manage this now in our heads. They were professionals dealing in millions of gold coins, but it was too difficult.

There are examples from Chinese and Japanese history to illustrate this, but these are two from European history. We're meant to find something which we can't yet see in ourselves; we have to have faith in the teacher who tells us, as the teacher has faith in us.

We're asked to make sacrifices, tremendous sacrifices. A man was complaining to a teacher about this; he said, 'We're asked to give up so much.'

The teacher said, 'Well, not necessarily, you know.'

And he said, 'But we are; we're asked to give up all these things.'

So they went to a judo *dōjō* where the

teacher knew the pupils and he called one of them out. He said, 'This boy's very keen. He's determined to become county champion.' And he asked him how he trained.

'I train three or four hours every evening, and Saturday nights I often run all night,' and this and this and this.

The teacher said to him, 'But you're making the most colossal sacrifices. I mean, you're so exhausted that you never go out to the cinema or anything like that in the evenings; no parties; you've got to keep off the drink which some of your friends are going in for. You have to sacrifice all this. Don't you feel it's sometimes too much?'

And the boy just looked at him and said, 'What are you talking about? I want to do judo!'

He's doing what he wants to do with his whole being. All these other things are simply peripheral, futile, boring.

The pupils, when they enter a school to learn the Way, sometimes complain that they are given a standard discipline that everybody's given, and it's a great disappointment.

A pupil says, on entry, 'We're all different, so I expect to have what will suit my character.'

So the Master of Novices says, 'Well,

these practices *will* suit your character.'

'Oh, good.'

And then the Master says, 'It's probably better if you don't talk to other people about them.'

'Ah yes.'

Of course, after he had been told that, he would never say a word, but somehow it leaks out, and then he discovers that in fact this is a practice that everybody is given. And so he goes to complain. 'Look, this is just sort of mass-production, isn't it? But it's got to *suit*; we're all different, aren't we?'

'Well, here we find that we're all the same.'

'But look, everybody says we're all different.'

'The fact that everybody says so, means that we're all the same.'

One word more about applying things to ourselves. Two women pupils studied under a woman teacher for whom they had a great reverence. She used to see them every week together, and one of them said coming away, 'You know, it's funny, at the end she always says something about egoism, or pride, or something like that.'

'Yes I've noticed that and I try to examine my conduct. And I generally do find that there is something in it, and I try to amend it.'

'Oh well, of course, you must speak for yourself. I've nothing to say about that at

The heavy burden of ego
drives the footsteps deep into sin.

all. But *me*, I do all that work for the temple; I never call attention to it; I never ask for any acknowledgement or any recognition (and I don't get any either). How could anyone think *I* was egoistic? Why, I'm well known for remaining in the background; I'm *famous* for my love of obscurity!'

THE STONE SERMON

THE STONE SERMON

In the Lotus Sutra (one of the old ones), there's the sort of Buddhist prodigal son. He's not actually prodigal; he wanders away from the king's palace when he's small, and forgets. And he wanders back again when he's much older — as a beggar. The king recognizes him from the palace and sends out a guard to bring him in. But the beggar, when he sees the guard, runs away. The king then has to take him on in the humblest capacity in the farthest corner of the kingdom, and gradually promote him up and then, finally, he declares, 'You are my son. You are the heir, and everything here is yours.'

The son has always been the heir to great power and wealth, but because he's a beggar and has forgotten his inheritance and who he is, he's afraid, although invited to come and claim it. Now, he has nothing.

When he sees the guard — he knows what guards do to beggars; if they simply move them on that's very lucky, so naturally — he runs away. If he had something, some little money, something to show, some sort of status, then he might be able to go with the guard without fear into the palace where he would be recognized.

These little pieces which I'm offering, are only words. There's nothing real there, so in a way they're sort of imitation money; they're imitation pearls cast before someone — perhaps only one person — who thinks that he's a beggar. And it might give him the courage and the faith to make the jump and go direct to the palace.

The title is *The Stone Sermon*. Outside many temples in Japan, there is a stone statue of the Bodhisattva Jizō, represented as a child of about six years old in a robe with very long sleeves. No crown or anything like that. The child has a rod with some rings in one hand, and a rosary, and it's all stone.

When a temple is built, it may be very magnificent. It's generally made of wood, and inside there may be many beautiful Buddha images of wood and metal, splendid golden decorations — but outside there is the stone child — Jizō. When the rain comes, he's not under a shelter. When the storm comes, he's exposed. When thieves come, they may steal anything from the temple, but the stone is too heavy to carry away. When the temple's burnt to the ground, all the artistic wonders in it — the paintings, the wooden sculptures and Buddhas of wood — become ashes; the Buddhas of metal are melted; all that remains is the stone Jizō. If you have seen a temple after a great fire, there's this one thing standing.

The image is speaking to us; there is something in us which is unmoved, untouched by storm, by fire. What would that be? Something that can't be stolen away by thieves; can't be struck by lightning. There's a message for us.

Part of the message is this: that the stone Jizō will outlive the temple, will outlive the wooden images and the decorations. We can say, 'Well, how does this apply to my life?' A historical example is Bodhidharma who went to China by sea and founded Zen there. An Indian tradition says that he was persecuted in India and almost driven out, and that after he was driven out, Buddhism began to decay. Tradition in China says that when he went to them, those who had the spiritual eye recognized him, but those who did not, saw their interests threatened, and they persecuted him. It's said that they tried to poison him six times and six times he stopped eating; six times they bribed the cook or perhaps threatened the cook, or they'd got one of their own men in as a monk to act as cook, and six times he stopped eating. He lived to the age of a hundred and twenty. The poisoners all died — of old age. He outlived them like the stone Jizōs, outliving the storms, outliving the fires, outliving the temple, outliving the people.

A sermon which I heard in Japan likened this message, this stone sermon, to a mountain. And the preacher said, 'A mountain attracts storms and rain. Rain comes down on the mountain — with lightning, with thunder — pouring rain onto the mountain. The peak of the mountain is above it, but the slopes, the sides of the mountain, are attacked by the storm. Attacked, yes; but when the storm has passed over, the mountain slopes are very fertile, and the streams which run down from the mountain, water the land for a long way around.' Then he said, 'Spiritual eminence attracts envy and venom and spite and persecution, but there is something which is above them. Still they come, but the end result of that persecution will be that the teaching will become very fertile and will give life to many people and to a large area.'

The stone, what else is the stone telling us? Jizō, the stone child, is represented in stone, but he's active sometimes and goes into the hells with his long sleeves. The guardian demons can't, of course, stop a Bodhisattva going into the hells. There is a hell in which the souls find themselves to be small children. They're on a sort of river bank with a lot of stones and they're building up little pagodas of stones. They're not sure why they're building them up, but there's a general impression among the children that if they can get them high enough, somehow they'll get out of this hell. And when the pagodas are getting quite high, a demon rushes out with an iron rod and knocks them down — then they start up again.

Well, this is a parable of our life. We feel, if we pile things up enough, somehow it'll get us out of hell. Just a little bit more. Some people's pagodas are very big: they've got name, they've got reputation, they've got a lot of money and influence, but still they feel there's something more to be added to their pagoda — they're not out of hell. Then, just as they're about to achieve, as they think, their objective, something comes and knocks it all down.

Jizō enters that hell and he sees the babies building their little pagodas. The demon guards — their teeth are grating together, but they pass him through — they must! He goes in and as he passes among the children, he stuffs some of them into his long sleeves. Then he comes out with his

face as good as gold, like when we're children and we've got a sweet in our mouth
and we just stand before our parents: 'Have
you been eating chocolate?' We shake our
heads, 'Oh no!' The guards can't challenge
him. They look at those bulging sleeves . . .
Seems a bit funny . . . But they can't
search him. And he goes out. The Jizō can
take the souls from this hell of meaningless
effort, and can rescue them.

Another lesson from the Jizō is this. He
stands in front of the temple by the wayside
with his staff and his rosary and his child's
face. And the people come, and the people
go. It's a figure of blessing. But he never
interchanges any remarks or greetings with
them; they pass by. Now, there is a practice in Buddhism of watching the passing
thoughts. One method of practising this is
to take oneself to be the Jizō, the stone
Jizō, unmoving, blessing, and the thoughts
coming and going. There's no interchange of
greetings, no arguments, no recognition as
they pass. They come and he blesses them
all equally without moving.

Well, this is the first little section on
the stone sermon. The illustrations (they're
taken from various sources) show how this
one thing, if it's meditated on, will begin to
speak to us — the stone, this image, will
begin to speak to us.

In the fourteenth century in Japan, one
of the great generals wanted to take a Jizō
image with his army. It was a famous

image, and he had the idea that if this was taken along with him, his strategies would be successful. So he applied to the temple, interviewed the abbot, and asked for permission to take the Jizō. The abbot said in a polite way, 'This will be meaningless and useless for you.'

The general said, 'But this Jizō has a great reputation and I believe in him, and I would like to take him with me.'

'If you take the stone image with you, you will take nothing. This is not the way to take Jizō with you.'

'Well then, how do I do it?'

'Find the Jizō standing in your own heart — a child, six years old, the staff and the rosary — then you take him with you.'

Now the next section. A saying of the Way is this: 'When you do a right action, don't cough!' When I put a gold piece as an offering, I mustn't flourish it. Don't cough when you do a good deed, to call attention to it.

There's always a tendency to fix on something; we want to have some one definite thing. The great Lotus Sutra, to which I referred earlier, has a great name as a sutra. The name, the reputation, the majesty and the sort of magic of the sutra leads gradually to the feeling that *this* is the one, and this is the *only* one. Provided there is a name and a fixed thing which we can practise and rely on — this is definite, this is clear — then there's a great tendency for the mind to go to that: nothing else matters — this is what matters. To know the name is very important and this means to have a concept also.

Now, there are about forty thousand different Chinese characters in the total Chinese language. Nobody, of course, can possibly know them all, but they exist. The ordinary educated person knows, or used to know, some four thousand, and then the specialists know one or two thousand in addition, in their own field, by which they recognize each other like magic passwords. Of course the Bodhisattvas in China know them all, and the Devil knows them all too! He's been around, and he has got these forty thousand off. Or he thinks he has.

One of the ways of baffling the Devil used to be seen occasionally in rural Japan. The Devil comes along. He comes to a house and he sees the name of the owner, which has to be put up outside. Then sometimes there's a devotional tablet with a spell, or something like that too. He sees the name and he sees the tablet and he knows what to do to get in. If their actions are not consistent with what's on that devotional tablet, he can get in.

The trick was to write up the name in ordinary characters, but on the devotional tablet to write very complicated signs that *looked* like Chinese characters, but in fact weren't; they simply looked like extremely complicated Chinese characters.

The idea was that the Devil comes along, reads the name, 'Oh yes, now the tab . . . Oh! can't read that! This must be the home of some *incredibly* learned and probably holy man, and it would be very dangerous for me to try to get in because I can't read the spell.'

So he passes on. But of course there's nothing there at all and the idea is to fool the Devil by his liking for something definite.

Now, the Lotus Sutra was regarded by several sects in Japan as the one definite and reliable thing. One of the sayings that was going round Japan about the fourteenth century (and for all I know still is), was that in these degenerate days the dharma has become polluted. Therefore though people try to attain the dharma from all sorts of traditional sources, it's polluted, it's been poisoned, and so Buddhism is falling deeper and deeper into degeneration and decay. So the dharma must be strained through the Lotus Scripture, and then all the defilements will be strained off and you will have the pure dharma. So study the Lotus Sutra alone!

Well, this was being said and a man — it doesn't say he was of the Lotus Scripture persuasion; perhaps he was just a man who thought he'd like to have a little bit of fun — took this idea to a Zen master and said to him, 'The Lotus Scripture, people are saying now, "The dharma has become polluted and the only way to get the true dharma is to strain it through the Lotus Scripture and strain off all the impurities." Do you agree with this in your Zen sect?'

'Oh yes, it's a fine teaching. Just one more thing — strain off the Lotus!'

He meant, it is a fine thing, the practices, but the idea that *this*, and *this alone* contains everything, must be strained off.

We tend to get carried away by irrelevances. I'll tell you one personal story here. I knew a very learned Sanskrit and Pali scholar who had studied the languages from the philological point of view. Gradually he became interested in what was *in* these languages as distinct from the grammar and the borrowings of the vocabulary from the Dravidian and other sources. He asked me whether I could suggest any teacher or place to go to study Indian Buddhism or Vedanta. He didn't much care which it was, so long as he did some of this training that he'd been reading about.

Looking at him, I advised him, 'On no account study Indian Buddhism, or Indian Vedanta.'

He was very surprised at this, 'What, then?'

'Study Japanese or Chinese Buddhism.'

'But I already *know* many of the Sanskrit and Pali texts; I know a great deal of the history; I know a lot of the Indian Buddhism, and you're saying, leave all that.'

And I told him that, in my opinion anyway, if he took a teacher of the actual practice, every time the teacher opened his mouth, he (that great scholar) would be criticizing, because if the teacher, for instance, came from Bengal, he would be pronouncing *maitrī* as *moitrī* (it's the way they pronounce it in Bengal); and every time the teacher exhorted him to practise friendliness, the first of the *Brahma Vihāras* — *moitrī*, he would feel, 'Oh dear . . . oh! that hurts . . . oh!' He would not be thinking Friendliness, he would only be thinking that it was a mispronunciation of *maitrī* and a replacement of that diphthong with another diphthong which doesn't and can't exist in classical Sanskrit at all. Then again, when the teacher said that *maitrī* is the first of the *Brahma Vihāras*, the four *Brahma Vihāras* which are supposed to be very ancient in Buddhism, instead of thinking of these four *Brahma Vihāras* — Friendliness, Compassion, Cheerfulness with somebody who's happy, and Indifference to someone who's evil —

instead of thinking of those four, he'd be thinking, 'Oh no! these aren't Buddhist in origin at all; they're found in the First *Pāda* of Patañjali's *Yogasūtradarśana* — the teacher is wrong!' He would not be thinking of the content, but only of the pronunciation, only of the historical associations. 'So much better,' I said to him, 'to study Chinese or Japanese Buddhism where you'll know nothing whatever, and you can come forward like a child, and actually learn something.'

Instructions are given, and often we can't understand the reasons. So sometimes reasons are invented to satisfy the mind of people who begin to practise, if they're such that they demand reasons for everything. There are many practices for which only experience can tell one the reason for the form of it. But the intellect, especially of people who are proud of their intellect, demands an explanation. Well, in judo sometimes, when we explain a technique to Japanese students, they will accept it and practise it for a few months; then, when they've got experience in that movement, we can explain why the hand's turned this way and not that way — then they can understand it. But with Westerners, the moment we say, 'Turn it this way,' they say, 'But why not that way? Wouldn't that be better?' Well, it's only experience that will provide the true reason, but we have to invent a series of sort of pseudo-scientific explanations which are not really true, but which satisfy them enough so that they can practise, and then later on they'll find out the true reason.

When I was very small (I can still remember it), about four years, I went into the kitchen and they had one of those big kitchen clocks which go Tick-tock, tick-tock, tick-tock. And I can remember asking my mother, 'What's it saying? Why does it do that?'

Well, now, it's not so easy to explain — Tick-tock — that's what it says. But I was the third son, so she had experience of this sort of question. She said, 'Oh, it says Tick-tock because it likes that.'

'Oh! doesn't it say anything else? Why doesn't it say anything else?'

And then, again ingeniously, she said, 'You know your drum; you like just banging it don't you? (Yes, God, how you like banging that drum, just banging it!) Well, it's the same: the clock likes saying Tick-tock.

I understood that. Yes — I liked beating my drum, and it liked going Tick-tock, on and on and on. It was a good reason.

Recently I've had a similar experience. Then, I couldn't understand the mechanism of the clock or why this sound would happen, and now I have a small computer the mechanism of which I don't understand, and I have a lesson once a week. My computer has one anomaly — in one operation you have to manipulate it in a way contrary to what the textbook says. When this first came up I said, 'Oh, but the textbook says *that*; why do we have to do *this*?'

And I could see the fellow (he's a young fellow who teaches me), I could see him thinking, 'y-e-s.' And then he said just what my mother had said, 'It likes that!'

We're given all sorts of practices and disciplines, and our intellect, especially if we're a bit lazy, will put up all sorts of objections and so on. And it's worth remembering that it's unreasonable to expect explanations of these things which depend on experience. We must rely, not on our intellect justifying the practice, but on the experience of the teacher who gives it.

A teacher has pointed out that there's the instruction that in a Buddhist training you have to go on one straight line, keep to some one thing. And yet at the same time it says, 'You've got to accept things; you've got to be flexible . . .' And the example he gave was of a gyroscope, or spinning top. If you've played with one as a child, or you've seen a gyroscope spinning, you'll know that its balance is so perfect when it's revolving, that it can travel down a string on the little notch at the bottom and still keep its balance on the string. If it was not spinning it couldn't do that. It's revolving about its centre and it can keep a perfect balance on that string. If you blow, the gyroscope will bow, but it will come back to its balance; it will give way to passing things, but it'll come back very strongly to its point of balance again, and settle itself.

He said, 'In the same way, there is something in the training which keeps on the same line and keeps perfectly balanced, but at the same time it can adapt quite freely and softly to the impulses, the momentary impulses, from outside, and adjust to the circumstances. And then it will again resume its balance and go forward.'

Another teacher said, 'The gyroscope adapts gently, but comes back firmly.' And he added, 'It doesn't react forcefully.' He gave as an example of that, a man who's trying to calm a lake or even the waves in his bath. He wants the bath water to be calm and he tries smacking down the waves as they come up. The teacher said, 'That's like you trying to smack down your thoughts as they arise: you create new ones. But if, instead, you simply keep still and watch the waves, then they'll die down of themselves.'

SHINING VISION

He outsits the passions,
as Bodhidharma outlived his poisoners
who themselves died of old age.

Once Ananda asked the Buddha, 'How is it that out of all these countless worlds and all these countless people in this world, the Buddha is giving teachings just to us here? It seems sort of, well, arbitrary. How is that so?'

And the Buddha said, 'I want to write something. Get me a reed.'

So Ananda went down to the bank of the Ganges. (They pluck off one of those reeds and cut it diagonally and then they write with it.) The Buddha held up the reed and said, 'How many of these reeds do you suppose there are on this stretch of the Ganges?'

'Oh-h-h-h . . .'

'And how many do you suppose there are on all the rivers of the world?'

'It's inconceivable, unimaginable.'

'And how many do you suppose there are in all the countless worlds?'

'Oh, can't be thought of.'

'And yet here and now, *this* is the reed the Tathāgata is going to write with!'

There is a saying about Kōbō who is the founder of the Shingon sect in Japan and one of the master calligraphers. He lived AD 800 and his calligraphy is still today regarded as one of the greatest examples of this very highly developed art. (He invented one of the Japanese alphabets.) It says, 'This wonderful calligrapher does not choose his brush. Kōbō Daishi — Great Teacher Kōbō — doesn't choose the brush.'

There are several brushes there. Most of us, if we've got to write something, have a good look at the brushes, choose the best one and reject others. But Kōbō is the great master and he can write a masterpiece with any of them, however imperfect. 'Kōbō doesn't choose the brush.' He just picks one up and writes the masterpiece with that.

It's extended to mean that we're not to think that, because we're not endowed with great intellect, with great power in the world, with great political adroitness, with great artistic talents, we can't manifest the dharma.

If I begin to think I have great talents, well, then I become a target.

If I begin to think I can't be bribed . . . Perhaps not now, there's nothing much I particularly want. And nobody's trying to bribe me . . . But . . .

A judo champion was offered a quarter of a million pounds to become a professional wrestler. That would today be nearly a million. He accepted, and the whole of the judo movement cried, 'Oh! how disgraceful!' He had to be expelled from the judo movement which strictly forbids public performance for money.

But when we were all saying how disgraceful it was, we were not being tempted ourselves. Supposing somebody offered me half a million pounds. Well, I'm very comfortably placed. I live in one big room; I sleep in a bunk above the kitchen, but I've got a rear balcony overlooking the garden of a very pleasant place. But confronted with that amount of money, I should start to think, 'Yes, with half a million . . . No! I reject that absolutely!!' And then I think, 'Well, I wouldn't mind a dog. I'd like a dog; I'd like a big dog — a Chow or an Alsatian — and that would mean a garden.' Of course, as I am now, I can't afford a garden. There's no temptation at all. But if I'm offered half a million . . . I could afford a garden, and somebody to exercise the dog.

And then, who knows? I stand straight now: I can't be bribed. And perhaps the cosmic Archer will aim and — pyoo-oo-ooh!

Another case. I can't be accused of undue aggression or anything like that. There's old Cumberbatch at the office, you know. He's an absolute Tartar, but gradually I've got patient with him. Now sometimes I even say, 'Poor old boy, he's, you know, he's getting past it so he's got to sort of exert himself and show himself off, and exercise his power in his last few years.' I'm getting patient, I'm getting forgiving. And then the cosmic Archer shoots: pyoo-oo-ooh!

The don't teach it now in judo, but they used to, when people got to a fairly high level; there are methods of killing people without leaving any mark or trace. It takes quite a lot of skill, but it can be done. Suppose I suddenly learn that, and have the skill. Now I look at old Cumberbatch — he's carrying on, and I suddenly think, 'You know, we could do without him!' Pyoo-oo-ooh! I've been shot.

The teacher tells us that we don't know what's in our own heart. Never think, 'I'm above that; I'm finished with that.' But don't get to feel crushed. Without any of those great virtues, or graces or talents — still 'Kōbō does not choose the brush'. The Buddha didn't *pick* a reed; he just took one that happened to be there. And in the same way, this large bell I have here is to tell people who aren't here, who don't want to listen, about Buddhism. I can go out and I can ring it; I can ring Buddhism into their ears and perhaps they'll listen. But tomorrow somebody'll be ringing another bell in the other ear. And then they'll move off it. The dharma doesn't have to be a great noise. People today are starving. We think, 'Oh yes, they're starving just for food.' No! they're starving for a spiritual training too. The people who are throwing bombs are not starved of food, but they're starved of a spiritual vision. And the teacher says, 'When people want to hear, even the tiniest bell will convey the dharma — to people who *want* to hear.'

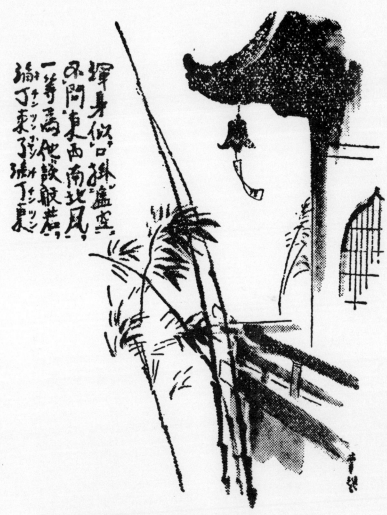

The whole body like a mouth, hanging in emptiness,
Not asking whether the breeze be from north or south,
   east or west;
For all alike declaring the Prajna wisdom —
Ti-ting-tung-liang, ti-ting-tung!

TIPS AND ICEBERGS

TIPS AND ICEBERGS

As you know, the iceberg is supposed to be ten per cent, or one per cent some people say, on the surface and the rest is hidden. My method of presentation here (it's not the only one) is to present just a small proportion and people can find out the rest of the iceberg. In this method of teaching, a number of illustrations or stories are given, but they're meant as, so to speak, seeds to work on. And unless they change our lives, then they're just entertaining stories. I'm telling these stories because some of them have been helpful to me and so I have confidence in them. But it's necessary that, like a seed, it should go into the ground.

You know the parable of the sower in our Christian Bible. There's a famous painting of 'the sower went forth to sow' which has been adopted as the sort of crest by

Iwanami, one of the most famous Japanese publishers. It shows the sower with the pannier of seeds and he's just scattering them broadcast, without looking. But that's not, in fact, the way you sow. You make a furrow in the ground and you put the seeds in. So this is one of the riddles, one of Christ's riddles, to which he didn't give answers. But it's one method of presenting, just by throwing out many different things, and perhaps the ground will open — be opened perhaps through a crisis — and it will receive one of those seeds. In the seed there's a potentiality which can grow without limit. From that tree, or plant, other seeds can come. Without limit it can grow, but it *has* to be received; it *has* to be something which can change our lives.

Suppose I'm living under a dictatorship, a ruthless dictatorship to which I've been sent perhaps by my country. Now, I see something very pathetic. Perhaps I can help by breaking the law a little bit to relieve that terrible suffering. Well now, I do so. Then I hear that the police are looking for the person who did this — it's been successful, the distress has been relieved — but they're looking for someone. They can't trace it to me, I know that. And I hear that they're making enquiries about someone else, whom they don't like. Perhaps they're going to arrest him. Now what do I do if they arrest him? I ask the wise old Minister, perhaps, at the embassy. I tell him, and then ask, 'What should . . . ?'

'Well, of course you've done wrong, but as a human being I must admit you did right. But if they arrest that chap, you can't do anything. And you'd better go home now.'

I say (in a low voice), 'But I should go and say that *I* did this — if they arrest him, that is.'

He shakes his head, 'No! it wouldn't do any good at all. They never let a man go once they've arrested him. It would simply mean two of you dying in jail.' He's given me an out, as they say today.

I think, 'Well, what am I going to do? If I go home, I may spend my life thinking that, owing to something I did, another man has been arrested and died. If I stay and resolve, "Well, if he is arrested, I'll confess, although it does no good," then I shall be living on top of a high diving board — every morning thinking, "Perhaps today, perhaps today — torture and death."'

Only two alternatives, both of them agonizing. Now, something has to arise which is different from those two. We can say, 'But there are only two. Either you can escape without saying anything, or you can make up your mind, if he's arrested, you'll confess. A terror, but you'll do it.'

But there's something else.

The purpose of these stories is that there's a seed in them which, if it's developed, will at a time like that, suddenly show itself. We can say, 'Oh, we don't have crises like that in our lives.' But we do. We all have these moments of agonizing and important choices when both sides are equally disastrous and we don't know what to do. We choose one side and always have the agony of knowing about the other.

Somebody I know is in great distress in this country; I haven't got enough money to help, but (as it happens) I'm momentarily in a position where I could successfully sneak it from my huge company which makes enormous profits. They would never know, and I could pass the money on. If I do so, how can I ever speak about honesty again? If I don't do it, I've left that person in terrible distress. Such things . . . And these stories have something in them.

The tip of the iceberg. As we know, the tip is ice and the huge mass which is concealed is ice. The tip's not quite the same as the iceberg in nature. Some of it's got a bit of snow on it, might have a couple of penguins or a polar bear, but in general it's the same above the surface and below the surface. But with us human beings, us human icebergs, it can be sometimes a little bit different, a little bit deceptive.

A British civil servant I knew was very high up, a man of great integrity of character, and a very hard worker and a very good fighter. He retired. In his retirement he decided to develop his interest in Christianity. He attended the church and did a tremendous lot for it. Then he discovered that there were some small things in the service which were not strictly traditional. So with his enormous energy and integrity he discovered the right way of doing the service, and then he sought to impose this on the congregation, which he finally did by giving everyone hell, until the vicar and the congregation finally agreed, 'Well, all right! We'll do it your way; it's no doubt right.' He won.

Then he fell very ill, and a friend visited him in hospital. The friend saw that this fighting face had now become peaceful. The old man was facing his imminent death brave as a lion — he was in peace.

And he said softly, 'You know, I feel I've fought the good fight. Now I know my life is coming to its close and I'm at peace in the Lord; I'm in the peace of the Lord.'

Well, of course, when anyone says anything like that to you and you're rather busy yourself, you can't help feeling, 'Well, I'd like to test this peace.' So the friend said to him, 'Well, Dan, old boy, this is marvellous you know; you're at peace. But here you are in bed. Supposing, while you're, er, laid up, they decide to change the service back again.'

'No, they promised me they wouldn't do that.'

'But they could, couldn't they?'

The old man reared up and shouted, 'I WILL FIGHT IT WITH EVERY FIBRE OF MY BODY!!' And then, 'Uhh!' and he slumped back exhausted.

Well, this was a case where the tip had become peaceful, but underneath that iceberg there was the old lion spirit; and such a situation can be quite a deceptive thing.

Then sometimes you can get a rather unexpected case. I know nothing of the history of China, but I was once pushed onto a radio discussion panel between four journalists about modern China, Chairman Mao's China. They had asked my colleague at the BBC of the Chinese Service who was an expert on Chinese history to join them. He fell ill at the last minute and the Producer said, 'Well, you know Japan, so you must know China.'

I said, 'No I don't! I know only two things about China.'

'Well, that's enough. Please go on.'

Well, I went there — it was a bit embarrassing. They talked about modern China. The Chairman introduced me. He said, 'Of course he's the Head of the Japanese Service, but I'm sure he'll say very interesting things to us about China.' And I just had to simply nod while they talked about modern China. Then they spoke about Chairman Mao perhaps becoming almost like a new emperor. And they spoke about the Communist system: 'Was this unique or . . . ?'

At this point I produced one of my two facts, I said, 'The fact is, the whole Communist sytem was tried in China several hundred years ago under Wang An-shih, and it lasted only about twenty years.'

There was a dead silence as if someone had quoted the Bible. The Chairman coughed and said, 'Oh . . . thank you.' Very impressed.

Then the discussion went on and I just looked judicial. And then they returned to the point about Chairman Mao: 'Could he become a new emperor, in some way?'

So then I produced my second piece of information. I said slowly, 'Well, you see . . . ,' (as if I was thinking about a lot of facts and then had chosen one), 'Now you take our game of Western chess — it's between a white king and a black king, and they fight, and one side wins. And this is the way the dynasties have replaced each other in the West — one king fights another king. But in Chinese chess, they don't have two kings; it would be inconceivable to the Chinese mind that the conqueror could become a new king. No, the contest is fought between the king and a general.'

Well, then there was another hush and I didn't have to say any more — there couldn't be two emperors; that's inconceivable to the Chinese mind. It was quite irrelevant to their point — but still they were impressed.

And at the end of the discussion, the Chairman thanked us all and thanked me. He said, 'We felt most impressed by your scholarship,' and so on, 'and we felt as though it was only the tip of the iceberg.'

It was. There are a lot of cases like that. We're swimming around holding up a little tip, and there's no iceberg underneath it. The visible form can be very convincing, but there may be no iceberg; it may be just tip. And the tip is shouting, 'Watch out for my iceberg!'

There's a traditional Japanese farce called *Changing Zazen*. Such farces are played between the serious Kabuki plays and are generally about some local lord, who's always depicted as an absolute fool; it's very democratic. Anyway, in this one, the local lord wants to go to the red light quarters, but he's completely under the domination of his wife. So one day he says to her, 'Enough of my dissolute ways, so contrary to the Buddha's teachings. I'm going to change and every week I'm going to sit all night in zazen,' (formal sitting meditation).

Now, the Japanese monks adopted from

China, for the winter, a long wadded meditation robe with a hood, to keep out the
cold. The wife said, 'I shall be looking in on
you, you know.'

'Of course!'

We see him get into this robe at the
beginning of the night and she sees him into
it.

Then she goes to see her sister for ten
minutes, and the lord does a switch with his
servant. He says, 'You've got to sit here all
night in this robe while I go out.' So the
servant has to do this and he sits there.

She comes back, looks in from time to
time, and sees this figure — perfect form!
And she gets rather impressed.

At about two in the morning she comes
in with some tea and she says, 'Husband, it
must be terribly cramped under there; just
break for a little bit and have this tea.'
The figure doesn't move. Well, then she
begs, 'You can have just a *tiny* little break;
they do in the monasteries; they have tea.'
Well, of course, in the end she pulls . . . and
she sees it's the servant. It all comes out.
Then *she* sits under the robe.

He comes back in the early morning
semi-drunk, and he sees, as he thinks, the
servant sitting there and he says, 'I've had a
marvellous night. I'll tell you all about it.'
And this thing just sits there. He says, 'You
needn't sit like that now; it's all right.' But
it just sits there. And he begins his story.

Well, we the audience can see under the

hood when it's a bit lifted up. He doesn't notice because he's drunk and he's telling his story, but we can see under the hood, a terrible face! Then — well, I won't tell you what happens when the cloak comes off, but the point is there is this form, perfect form, of meditation. In the first case the lord is doing it to get an advantage; in the second case the servant's doing it because he's *got* to; and in the third case, when she's sitting there, it's a demon. Now, this is used as an illustration of wrong ways of practising zazen. One can practise it to get an advantage; one can practise it because one feels one's got to; and one can practise it, sometimes, because one is a sort of demon. The form is the same.

Another point is our judgment. We judge a spiritual teaching, or perhaps a spiritual teacher, and we judge on our own basis. There are a number of Eastern stories on this, but there are also some from the West.

We can't recognize in others what we don't at all have in ourselves. How could we? We must have it to some extent ourselves to recognize it.

Some French scientists at the beginning of the century decided to test whether an elephant was musical. So they went to the zoo and they took a violinist with them who played a bravura passage from a composer whom was thought by the scientists to have been one of the top composers of the end of the eighteenth century — Monsigny. The violinist played this, and the elephant listened for a bit, then yawned and turned away. The scientists concluded: the elephant is not musical.

But as a matter of fact, today, pretty well no one's heard of Monsigny. And most of us, if a bravura passage from Monsigny was played on the solo violin, would probably yawn and turn away.

So perhaps the elephant had the best of it. The scientists weren't particularly musical. They just chose a name that happened to be admired in France at the time, whose music we now think very little of, and they concluded — because they were not musical themselves — that the elephant couldn't be musical. Well, in the same way, people who lack spirituality will not be able to recognize the spirituality in the teacher. We can be put off by something irrelevant.

I give an example from my own experience. A judo man was extremely expert at a particular small branch of technique — he was very, very, good at it. He wasn't an official teacher, but he used to go nearly every day to the Kōdōkan and would practise that, and teach people who wished to be taught. But he had something a little bit vicious about him. He used to — not injure people, he never injured anybody — but hurt them just a tiny little bit. And those who practised with him had this experience — he would just hurt, just a little bit — no damage at all.

Well, most people didn't like to practise with him, although there was so much to be learned from him about that particular branch of judo. After having this experience myself, I too thought, 'No, I don't want to learn from that man; he's a bit vicious.' Then I argued with myself, 'But he's very good at that technique; you could learn technique from him that would be difficult to find elsewhere, he's so expert at that.' Again the thought came, 'No, I don't want that; he's vicious; he might infect me with his viciousness.' And then I thought, 'Am I ever vicious? Well no, I can't be because I'm sort of disgusted by his viciousness.' And finally I thought, 'Well, I don't know; I might be; *I* might infect *him*!' Then I decided to practise and learn from him.

Now that man's viciousness was an unpleasant characteristic, but it had nothing to do with my learning technique from him. I finally realized I was being put off by something quite irrelevant.

In the same way, people coming to a spiritual path have to decide what it is that they want and not be put off by things which basically don't matter. Things from outside can put us off. Things from outside can encourage us. But while they're all still from outside, they don't really solve any problem at all.

The Accountant who comes every year to do my income tax brings a printer-calculator. He sits there going through the papers while I try and work on translation on the other side of the room. (I have to be there to answer any question, and I've got only one room.) And it goes, bzzz . . . bzzz, bzzz . . . bzzz, bzzz, bzzz, bzzz, bzzz. I think, 'Well, that's the last.' And then there's silence for a bit and then, bzzz . . . bzzz, bzzz. And I think, 'Oh . . . what a nuisance.' I get on somehow, but it's annoying. Now he's rather perceptive and he said to me, 'You know, every time this buzzes, you'll be paying less income tax.' And suddenly it all changed — bzzzz, bzzzz, bzzzz — and I was thinking, 'Keep it up!' It was clever of him, but still it was from outside. And a solution from outside is ultimately no solution at all.

There are some examples not necessarily very elegant, but nevertheless striking. A stray dog runs up to the stone steps at the back of your house and makes a terrible mess there, and a fearful stench. You go out and look at it, 'Oh! disgusting!' Then you get some flower petals and you scatter them on top. 'Now, isn't that be-au-ti-ful?' But all the time there's that terrible stench.

This is a solution from outside by putting something outside onto it. It seems to solve the problem, it seems to make something beautiful, but all the time you know it hasn't. There's this awful smell that invades your house, and the real problem hasn't been solved.

The treasure has to be found in our own house, not brought from outside. While we put things on top, while we have outside thoughts and concepts and influences, we will never be established.

Most of us stand upright by looking at the verticals in the walls. While they're upright, we're balanced. They make special rooms in which the verticals (the doors and so on) are slightly on the slant, and people fall over because they're aligning themselves with what they think are verticals but which aren't. A trained judo man's balance is internal, and such a room doesn't affect him at all. But most people align themselves from something outside. No harm perhaps, physically, but spiritually, if we do that — if we align ourselves from something outside — we are always liable to collapse when the outside environment is twisted or abnormal. So the ultimate purpose of the teacher is not to provide you with true outer verticals of morality and so on to align yourself with, but to develop the inner sense of balance in yourself. We have to find something within ourselves.

When the Shinkansen, the so-called Japanese 'bullet train' first came in, it was a great triumph of technology, and a national triumph also. All the kids heard about it. And they arranged to have parties of the children from the country villages so that they could ride on this train. A teacher told me about one such party, where for some reason, some oversight, it was not explained to the children that they were going to ride on the Shinkansen, of which they'd seen so many pictures and photographs. So they got on this train without seeing the engine and they were shooting along, when they saw another one on another track. The children all crowded to the side of the train, 'Look, the Shinkansen! Look, the Shinkansen!' And the teacher said, 'Boys and girls, you're *in* the Shinkansen. This is it! You're in it. You don't need to look at that one over there. Look at what you're in.'

There's a treasure in our own house which often we don't see. We can say, 'Well, how can there be?' One of the Indian stories tells how the merchants in some of the towns (when India was the richest country in the world) were very strict about business ethics. And one man cut some corners. They used to expel such people from the city and stone them, not kill them, but stone them and then drive them away. They took everything he had, tied him to a stake outside the city, held back his wife and child, and threw stones.

A little boy, the son of one of the big merchants, was there — not often you get the chance to throw a stone at a grown-up! He picks up a sharp stone and he throws it. It catches the man on the face. It just misses his eye, and the blood pours down.

Well, then they release his wife and child, and all go away. The two of them rush to him and set him free. Now, he's got nothing, he's penniless, he's disgraced — in the sunset, the dying sun. He'll have to go to the next city. He might have some faint hope of an uncle somewhere, but it's a total destruction.

As he hangs his head and looks down, he sees a gleam; the ray of the dying sun makes a gleam — one of the stones. He bends down, picks it up and it's a great jewel. The rich merchant had a ring with a big jewel in it. In the excitement he must have knocked it somehow against a brick or something like that. It fell down and the little boy, not looking, just grabbed the sharp stone and threw it.

There is a Japanese poem:

The stones which were thrown at me —
When I picked it up,
One of them was a jewel.

This comes again and again. There's something hidden even in the terrible experiences we have, which, if we have spiritual sight and discrimination, we can find.

I'll read a little bit from a translation of a book which I did translate, all except this little bit; it's in *A First Zen Reader* and it's by Sessan.

There's an old saying in the Zen school:
'When you come to pick them up, the
very stones are gold.' When the eye of
the heart is opened and we see rightly,
the shattered tiles that have been
dropped on the road, are shining with
the gleam of gold. In our everyday life,
to recognize the true worth of every
little thing, every tiny fragment of what
we are using every day, to respect it —
that gives life real meaning. In the
daily life of Zen, everything is to be
made pure and exact and elegantly
simple. In our conduct — going, staying,
sitting, and lying down, as we say —
we're never to think of anything as trivial, but to find a great meaning in it. In
using one's personal things, we mustn't
use them casually, or forgetfully, or
wrongly, or mistakenly — they must be
used rightly. These days they talk about
consumables which, of course, is all
right, but it's not good to use for profit
the consumables, to acquire economic
advantage for oneself. Higher than use
for profit, is *loving* use of the things in
the right way; it means to love the
things we use. But even so, to love
things because they are pleasant and
because they suit me, still does not yet
get away from self-satisfaction. There
has to be proper *living* use. Then, for
the first time, there's life in the handling of the things and that's a very fine

thing. But it's not yet outside the sphere of practical wisdom. We have to go further and come to — *good* use of things. Now, for the first time, we come to follow the nature of the thing itself when we use it, and we come to live virtuously. Again one step: we must come to *pure* use; we must purify the things when we use them. Now it is that their religious meaning appears. Nowadays it's fashionable to use phrases like 'cleaning up society', but it's when we try to make things pure, uncontaminated, infinitely clear and noble as we use them, that the seeds of religious life are sprouting. Again a step: we must come to *spiritual* use; to spiritualize the things as we use them. Now it's not just a thing, not just a material substance, but it's of spiritual nature, spiritual essence, and it becomes radiant. 'When we pick them up, the very stones are gold.' The thing is a blessing, is precious — instinctively we find a gesture of reverence in ourselves.

This sort of example is given. Men shave every morning from their true face just a little almost imperceptible sprouting of beard. Now, if I don't shave that, then I may look very smart, I may be wearing evening dress, but every time I move my head, it'll rasp against the hard edge of the collar — very uncomfortable. I think, 'Oh well, I won't wear a hard collar; I'll wear a very soft Cashmere scarf.' But then the scarf catches on the beard stubble, and I find little bits of fluff all over my face. And what a relief to shave the face clear!

One of the teachers has said, 'Use the sharp edge of criticism to shave the conceit from the true face.' And when we're actually shaving, we're to feel we're shaving away our conceit and prejudices.

I sometimes have to translate Japanese poems in the texts which I do — they're not so easy. Sometimes the mediaeval prose is not easy either. And then some kind friends tell me, 'You know what so-and-so said? He said, "In one of those translations, Trevor's put 'neither of them are absolutely right.' But that's an elementary grammatical mistake in English. Poor old Trevor! It's not that he doesn't know Japanese, he doesn't know English!"'

Well, then I think, 'Oh! it's a trivial point; it's colloquial English. I disregard that; huh, I pay no attention to criticisms like that.' But gradually it yeasts up and I think, 'Well, you know, if you look at some of *his* translations, they're pretty careless aren't they? AND AS A MATTER OF FACT, HE WOULDN'T KNOW A POEM IF YOU HIT HIM OVER THE HEAD WITH IT!!!' Now my whiskers are sprouting, and (if I can do it) to shave them off with the sharp edge of that criticism, by accepting it, is a great relief.

This cloth here: it was quite a good cloth once, but it hasn't been cleaned and it hasn't been ironed, so it's got these persistent creases in it. Well, our minds are acquiring creases and dirt all our lives. However you drop this cloth, it'll always fall into the same creases. This other one's old and it's not quite clean, but it's been washed and it's been ironed. This can take any shape: I can polish with it, I can wave it, I can refold it in another shape, I can use it to tie something — it's free. Now our minds too get set into creases. 'I *always* do this. No, no! I *never* do that, no, no. *This*, yes; *that*, no.' 'I always look at things *scientifically*, you see.' And then other people say, 'No, it's to *feel*, to *feel*, that's all that matters.' A very intellectual man said, 'Some people are all for *life*, *life*, but I prefer reading.' These are creases. The spiritual training is purification — cleaning — and then ironing with a hot iron to take out the creases; then mind can fall into any shape needed, or be folded and put away.

This is perhaps the most famous poem in Japanese; it's one of these very short ones:

The old pond;
A frog jumps in;
The sound of the water!

This is a most famous poem and the whole of Japan resounded with it. Well then, it's said that one day the same poet was walking on the same path and he happened to pass this same old pond and he looked, and he saw a frog that seemed to be hanging about! It wanted to give an encore. Well, this is a satirical example of how when we've done something great or good, there's a tendency to want to repeat our effects. But the thing is — to go! They say, 'Do good!' And it's added to that, 'Do good and go!' And I've even heard it in the form, 'Do good and run!'

At a temple where I used to go sometimes, Sōjiji (one of the great training temples), I got to know the head monk who told me quite a lot of things, and one of them was this: 'If your mind's disturbed, or perhaps you're very bored, take a very slow deep breath in — till your lungs are quite full. Hold it just for a second, then very slowly let it out.' Well, some judo men are — or were — trained to observe the breath, and on another occasion when I was, as I thought, saying some rather interesting things to him, I noticed that he was very, very slowly breathing in. And in this hall at the moment, I seem to feel that the hall itself is somehow . . . So I'll finish. Thank you for your attention.

OTHER PUBLICATIONS BY
BUDDHIST PUBLISHING GROUP

THE ZEN TEACHING OF
INSTANTANEOUS AWAKENING
by Hui Hai
Translated by John Blofeld
Zen Master Hui Hai was of the same tradition as Hui
Neng, Ma Tsu and Huang Po. His teaching is very
direct and just as pertinent today in the West as it
was 1200 years ago in China.

BUDDHISM
A comprehensive account of Buddhism and its teachings, including meditation, karma, rebirth, advice on
treading the path, a survey of schools, and history, etc.

BUDDHIST MEDITATION
A straightforward guide to sitting and walking meditation.

REBIRTH
A Buddhist explanation of the processes of birth and
death.

ZEN GRAFFITI
Striking comments on truth.

ECHOES IN THE VOID
Companion to Zen Graffiti.

GREAT AWAKENING
Excerpts from the Dharma of
Ch'an Master Hsu Yun
Advice on realizing one's true nature through medi-
tation and the use of a koan.

THE OXHERDING PICTURES
A modern version of a Chinese Zen meditation guide in
verse and pictures.

THE DIAMOND SUTRA
The Buddha's teaching on being free from all notions.
A Buddhist classic.

THE PERFECTION OF WISDOM
IN 700 LINES
Translated by E. Conze
A dialogue between the Buddha, Manjusri and others on
how to realize perfect wisdom.

RELEASE FROM SUFFERING
A guide on how to find release from suffering through
awareness in everyday life.

TEN BUDDHIST FABLES
by John Snelling and Marcelle Hanselaar
Beautifully illustrated, eminently readable stories from
the Jataka Tales.

THE BODHISATTVA PATH
The path of the Buddha, the path of enlightenment.

TIBETAN WISDOM
Advice from two Tibetan gurus — Phadampa Sangay
and Jetsun-Milarepa.

Translations of Pali suttas by I.B. Horner:

THE SATIPATTHANA SUTTA
A detailed explanation of mindfulness, the basis of Buddhist meditation.

THE NOBLE QUEST
A biographical account of the Buddha's search for enlightenment.

THE PARABLE OF THE WATER SNAKE
The Buddha likens a wrong grasp of his teaching to taking hold of a poisonous snake by the tail.

THE FOUR NOBLE TRUTHS
Two suttas conveying the Buddha's teaching on the truth of suffering, its cause, and the way to overcome it.

CURRENT LIST
For our current list of publications, please send a stamped addressed envelope or an international reply coupon (available from post offices) to:

Buddhist Publishing Group
PO Box 136
Leicester LE2 4TZ
England